Wisdom of Wealth

MAVEN PRESS

Copyright © Laura Elizabeth
First published in Australia in 2023
by Maven Press
Roleystone WA 6111

Cover Design by Jennifer Birkhead

Edited by Jade Bell

All rights reserved. No part of this book may be used or reproduced by any means, graphic, electronic, or mechanical, including photocopying, recording, taping or by any information storage retrieval system without the written permission of the copyright owner except in the case of brief quotations embodied in critical articles and reviews.

Because of the dynamic nature of the Internet, any web addresses or links contained in this book may have changed since publication and may no longer be valid. The views expressed in this work are solely those of the author and do not necessarily reflect the views of the publisher and the publisher hereby disclaims any responsibility for them.

 A catalogue record for this work is available from the National Library of Australia

National Library of Australia Catalogue-in-Publication data:
Wisdom of Wealth/Laura Elizabeth

ISBN: 978-0-6456356-7-6
(Paperback)

ISBN: 978-0-6456356-8-3
(e-book)

ACKNOWLEDGEMENTS

In unity, we honour and pay our respects to the custodians of Whadjuk Noongar Boodjar country, the lands on which this book was first seeded.

We pay our respects to the Elders both past and present and to those emerging.

The stories within these pages may contain sensitive content and/or memories of loved ones who have passed on, which may activate a response within you.

Please read with awareness and care.

Contents

Julia Eddy
CONNECTIONS 1

Karen Weaver
MONEY IS ENERGY 9

Kelly Bowen
SEEKING WEALTH: A PATH TO PROSPERITY 16

Kim Kent
MONEY MATTERS 31

Laura Elizabeth
MINDFUL MONEY IN YOUR SLEEP 42

Lezly Kaye
THE MONEY MATRIX 50

Martha Hansen
ANCHORING WEALTH INTO YOUR ENERGY 60

Worksheets
WISDOM OF WEALTH 71

Julia Eddy

Connections

My name is Julia Eddy, and I am proud to be a businesswoman working as a sole trader in the NDIS. With over ten years of experience in community and government sectors, I was placed in an inconceivable position in 2021 that made me question my work and gave me an ultimatum.

Despite being in a job where I felt rewarded, successful and passionate, I found myself forced to decide to continue in a job I loved or resist the pressure to accept a vaccine that did not align with my beliefs or values.

Taking one of the greatest leaps of my life and going completely against the grain, I left a secure government position on a comfortable salary, losing relationships in the process. I now find myself in a six-figure business, working with people I align with, a flexible schedule to create my own rules and have created the life I envisioned.

I never considered myself a businesswoman, but recently, I've realised that I actually am. When you become a business owner, either in your spare bedroom at home or in a fancy office space, I think there is certainly the onset of imposter syndrome. I will safely say that it sits with you for at least the first year, if not more. The first-year rolls by, and you think, wow, I actually made it. When you're deep into that second year, curiosity starts to set in: is this really me running my own show?

I've always been a person who just gets in and gets it done. I never really ask for help, seek advice, or look to others for their opinion. I just do the work. Not too long ago, I had a moment of realisation that people were approaching me for advice, for help, and to seek my opinion. It's such a strange thing when people start wanting your thoughts. When I realised that they were coming to me to find a solution and I was making money, it was then that I accepted that I was a businesswoman!

I would love to share with you the key basics of a successful business. It's not complicated, but it works.

Make Connections

Business is made through connections—connections with people, connections with customers and, the most underrated connections, with other businesses. When you build solid relationships with those around you, you will be the first person they call for almost anything.

For those who are just starting out, be patient. Finding the right people you need to connect with who will bring you the results you seek will take time. However, with new connections comes great responsibilities. It's not just about the effort put into making contact. It's the time spent staying connected and building the foundation of trust, credibility, communication and reliability. If you are unreliable or fail to communicate, you will lose your connection and any future work as a result.

Great business people never stop looking for new opportunities that present better ways to grow their profits. In any interaction you have in your work or personal life, always present yourself in its best light, as you never know when a new opportunity may arise.

Wisdom of Wealth

Find a Mentor

You cannot do business alone. While you think you have all the answers and your confidence precedes you in your chosen field, someone will always know more. Inevitably, there will always be that one person who has done it all before and knows more than you at this phase of your business journey. Find them! Find that person you connect with, can have a professional relationship with, learn from, grow with and tap into. All coaches need coaches; it's the quickest way you will progress and the best chance of solid success.

Your business will thrive when you realise how important this step really is. It demonstrates your willingness to open yourself up to criticism and allow feedback. It will enable you to learn and accept the parts you need to change in order to be successful.

As business people, we have to continue to learn not only in our field but also in the way that we work. Often, it's only those who are looking in who can pinpoint the key areas of improvement and suggest change, but only if you are willing to accept it. When you speak to others, gather information and ask questions, it allows you to try things you may have never intended before and creates amazing outcomes. Make it your mission to broaden your toolbox of resources to one day pass on to those around you. Sharing knowledge breeds growth!

Make Mistakes

Although I still feel new to this world of business, I've also been in it a really long time. I had a business once, and it did not work out. Looking back, I thought that I let it fail me, but in reality, it's made me money in the future without even realising it.

My past business mistakes happened at the absolute best time to fail. In hindsight, it's what needed to occur to allow me to succeed in the right type of business and at the right moment.

If your expectations are that business is smooth sailing, turn around now.

Julia Eddy

While making mistakes can cost you time, money, and potential relationships, unfortunately, it is a necessary evil, at least to begin with. It's not the mistake that's important. It's how you manage it and understand what it can teach you for what lies ahead. I have learned that no one mistake ever goes to waste if you use it wisely. You must accept that it is likely to present itself again or that its learnings will allow you to prevent a much greater cost in the future. If you can learn how to handle a mistake efficiently and with great poise, you will become more refined as a business owner and even create changes in your personal life. Make sure you never let a mistake sit too long, deal with it, learn from it and move on.

Know Your Worth

When you do business, it's important to back yourself and the prices you charge. Be confident in what you do, and your consumer will never question your cost. If someone wants to debate the cost of your service or product, reducing your pricing is the quickest way to devalue your business. Remember, you win some and you lose some. It's better to lose that one person who doesn't believe in you enough to pay your worth than to devalue your product, your business and, even worse, devalue yourself. It is a very hard place to come back from, and you will find it will affect the longevity of your success.

It's simple: people buy from people they like. If you can produce the best product in the world, yet you can't make the consumer see its worth, you will never make a sale. Whether you are in the business of selling your services or selling an item, you must sell yourself first. Adapt your style to the consumer and find a way to give them no reason to say no.

Take Risks

Do things you never thought were possible. Dream big. As Thomas Jefferson said, 'With great risk comes great reward.' Set your sights on things that will take your business to the next level, things that will make you more money, and things that will make you the leader in your field. Calculated risks are needed for a business to grow. If you keep doing average things, you're bound to get average results. One of my favourite sayings by Ellen Johnson Sirleaf is, 'The size of your dreams must always exceed your current capacity to achieve them. If your dreams don't scare you, they aren't big enough.'

Make a Plan

I can guarantee that if your plan is to wing it in business, your plan is likely to fail. With everything you do or every idea you create, a plan must support it. From your daily schedule to your yearly budget, you must make a plan and follow it religiously!

When you're faced with a barrier to your plans in business, you must find a way around it. When you find yourself questioning what's achievable and reach a point where all feels impossible, find your 'workaround'. Every mountain has an alternative route, and everything that's broken can be fixed. It's your job to adapt and make it happen. If you always under-promise, you will never fail to over-deliver.

Keep Learning

Educate yourself and do it often. The day you find yourself with nothing new to learn is the day you need to change direction in your business.

There is no roof to learning.

There is no end to knowledge.

Always invest back into upskilling yourself and the people around you to achieve business growth. This creates opportunities not only for new information but potentially new connections. It's important to identify when it's time to outsource tasks so that you can spend more time working on your business rather than in it.

When you do things with consistency, you won't need to advertise. You won't need to market. The business will find you. You won't need to find

Julia Eddy

the business. It will grow organically. Consistency is the definition of great success, and when you hit the moment and your business flows, you know you've truly made it.

About Julia

Growing up in a small sugar cane town in Mackay, north Queensland, I couldn't find a way out fast enough. Seeking big city life, I packed up my two-door Mazda and spent the next few years in Brisbane working hospitality, with big dreams to travel the world. Soon after making enough money, I booked my first plane ticket out of the country and landed in Europe for six months of working and backpacking solo.

Returning to Australia, I moved to Melbourne, a place I would call home for five years. Finally, I became a travel agent, which I had always aspired to be, after completing several useless courses just out of high school. The first store I worked at was Smith St, Collingwood, a well-known area for Vietnamese food and its hipster culture to anyone who's spent time in Melbourne. I was then labelled the manager of one of the worst performing stores in the state, if not the country, to see out its lease while we waited to close its doors. In just one year, with a loyal team around

Julia Eddy

me, we turned that little store into the green zone of finances and turned a decent profit. I was making a name for ourselves as ones who could do the impossible and keep Collingwood open—years of travel sales left me sick of the long and stressful days. It was time to move on.

I'd always wanted to live in Dubai since I first visited back in 2006, and with a quick Google search, I found Emirates had an open day right there in Melbourne at the Hilton Hotel. Never ever wanting to be an air hostess, I applied for the job and found myself one of seven chosen from a room full of almost two hundred applicants on my way to the Middle East! Living in one of the world's tallest residential buildings on the twenty-seventh floor, I was in what most would consider a dream job, travelling the world and getting paid for it. After almost three years of living a high life, I needed a change. Curious about moving to Madrid or Singapore, I decided to go back to Mackay to reset and choose where I wanted to be next.

Close to ten years later, I have never left. I'm happily married with two kids, a vintage caravan and a thriving business. Training and fighting amateur muay thai has also become embedded in our lives. I am lucky to say I also get to continue to travel, work remotely, and still earn an income. I am excited about all the ways that I can continue to grow my business and adapt to the changes of the NDIS and for all of the learnings and opportunities that lie ahead.

Reach out via Facebook for all things NDIS:
Facebook: facebook.com/JuliaEddySupports

Karen Weaver

Money Is Energy

This chapter will share the story behind my success and how I made my million-dollar year happen. It was strategy, and it wasn't. It had a lot to do with flow. I'm going to share with you my knowledge and my life master gifts I live through and do every day. I never compromise my values because when I do, I'm compromising myself, and a little bit of me dies.

Every woman should show up for her ambitions and dreams and fill their own cup. When we do, we can pour the best of ourselves into others. Everyone around us benefits when we are our highest and best versions. I really want to emphasise at the beginning of this chapter that we don't need to compromise ourselves in the process of advancing, claiming and calling in money. Now, I want to touch on the idea of money.

Some so many people will read this book: good people, spiritual people, and people doing some really great things in this world. And money is important so that good people can do good things. We don't need all the bad people with the money. We need people with good intentions to keep the wealth flowing. It's important to remember that wealth and money are energy, and we need to put energy into finances because when we do, we can experience and create opportunities for others.

I regularly go into money energy. It's not an energy I love hanging out in for too long, but it's important, and I love the manifesting process. My manifesting process is where I set an intention. I call it in. I command it in. I honour the journey and have my inspired thoughts and opportunities in my peripheral vision activate, so when the message comes true and clear in my vision from the universe, I will be a hell yes and action it. It always requires courage as each step is revealed.

We don't need to know every step, but as each is identified, we need to have our souls connected with the journey. This way, we can acknowledge without a shadow of a doubt through the power of knowing that this is what we are meant to say yes to right now. And I don't see it as just a yes. It's a hell, yes! Hell, yes, this is what I need to do right now! That's what I need to do right now.

During my million-dollar year, I was so in the flow and enjoying what I was doing so much. I wasn't so much focused on finances but knew that the money flow was just circulating. It was beautiful. It was brilliant. I was winning awards; I was serving so well, and I'd done it all in service. It wasn't until my accountant pulled together our finances the following year that I discovered we had a million-dollar year. It was such a wonderful feeling. I took the opportunity to reflect on what the formula for my success and creating a million-dollar year was. Reflecting on 2012, two years after I wrote my first novel, I had set an intention to build a million-dollar press, and I made a sacred promise to go on an organic journey to allow that to come in. So, I showed up for the story every day.

I was so deeply connected with the journey that I got to know the hell yeses very easily, and I had to learn how to say no to the things my heart wasn't in. I learnt that the hell yes feeling was only when my heart was fully engaged. It's the feeling we get when we absolutely know it's the next thing we must do. We have a burning desire to make it happen. So, when an opportunity or something doesn't align with our intentions, we're distracting ourselves from the goal.

But most importantly, what we are doing is taking energy away from where we're going. And if you say yes to something your heart is saying no to, you're dulling your light, and you're dulling your flame, your glow and your impact. Your heart must be all in giving the best of yourself to the situation. You're actually doing a disservice to the person or the opportunity by saying yes if your heart is a no. So always say no to the hell nos and yes to the hell yeses.

I learned that lesson early on. I also identified that the energy, flow, and people coming to me aligned because I was so in flow and connected to where I was. I knew it wouldn't last forever because I was on an evolutionary journey. But I also knew that I could teach others and pass on that flow. It's all about the story because it doesn't matter if it's me helping stories into the world or others. It's all stories, and stories make the world go round.

Another thing I identified for that year was that I was really aligned with my values. I was writing *The Miracle of Intent* that year, book three in my series, and the energy in that book was amazing! I was getting up at 5 am to write. I love getting up that early. It's the best part of the day. I feel so creative and inspired. I accommodate for rising that early by going to bed early, but I always start the day doing something I love. That way, I'm beginning the day the best way I can, by writing. I love to write, and as a mother of six, I like to get ahead of the crazy, crazy mornings and do something for me. I rise early and fill my cup, then get into the day and get all the things that need doing done. There's always a never-ending list, but I don't stress about that.

Another thing I did in my million-dollar year was reinvest. Everything I made, I reinvested in growth, intentionally so, either visibly or in resources. As a wonderful friend of mine talks about, I sent the money out to make money babies and bring it back, which I love. One of the main things I had to do after that year was upgrade my mindset to a million-dollar mindset.

It's still a mindset of service and absolute loving intention because I am a great believer that loving intention is the super fuel of all success.

When you harness the love in your heart and apply it to anything, you can achieve your dreams. I can easily access love when I think of my children and my love for them. I use that love in all aspects of my life. There's a beautiful poem, or rather a big long affirmation by Louise Hay, called *I Love Myself*, and it really activated me when I listened. It realigns my core values and keeps everything centred, flowing and energetically vibrational. I wrote a quote today that I believe is very powerful. I will gift it to you in this chapter. It goes 'We are only one energetic sidestep away from our dreams.'

Just think about that for a moment. What is meant by that? What I mean is, energetically, if we're not attracting and money is not flowing, then we are not aligned on the path of receiving.

Even since having a million-dollar year, I've had those times where I've had to sidestep back into it. All it takes, though, is a reset, a reboot and a memory refresh to realign you.

You can do that through music or wherever you find joy, whatever lights you up. Maybe your future self-meditation is one that the wonderful Tara Mur does called *Meet Your Inner Mentor*, which is all about embracing your inner mentor to help you make clear professional and personal decisions. It's an amazing one for me because I get to connect with my higher self there, and my avatar guides me.

I love that meditation, and I no longer have to do the meditation to connect to my higher self. She's there, ready for me to ask questions, and it's a beautiful thing. And that's the higher version, the older version of me, who guides and shares and is the best version of me I can be. I see myself in her, and I see myself getting closer to her daily. And that is so special. And you can do that, too. You can really, truly do that and allow it to be your guiding light.

What do I mean by sidestep? I mean that sometimes we are on the right path, but we aren't energetically aligned with it. We're walking the right path, but our energy just isn't there. We need to keep the vibrations high, and love, joy and gratitude are the high vibrations. Energy and emotions make great things happen in our lives, and it's what we need to be in the flow of receiving. Any virtuous things have a high vibrational impact and will attract amazing things—the mindset of service. It's your job to keep yourself happy. Be joyful with all your heart. Allow yourself to experience love.

Love takes courage because a lot of us have been hurt during our lives, and it leads us to shield our hearts. Hurt makes love a difficult emotion to access. But when you can capture the essence of love and allow yourself to access it, it's like firing up a burner within yourself, and that will attract anything that you want at super speed. I call it the super fuel to success because love fuels success. Why do you think it's always talked about? If you look at ancient rich cultures, love is at the forefront. They use it as a super fuel. It's not just about loving. It's about harnessing the essence of that love and applying it to your actions, so doing everything with loving intention.

You're getting all my wisdom here, but I want to share another thing in closing. On any journey you pursue, there's always going to be growth, and when there's growth, there are always challenges. I always speak about H. R. Moody's book, *The Five Stages of the Soul*. I always talk about stage three and stage four, which is the struggle and the breakthrough, because so many people bail in the struggle and never make it to the breakthrough.

The struggle period is when you've done everything you need to do. You've answered all the inspired thoughts, and you are there in that waiting period, waiting zone. And it's uncomfortable because things are growing and shifting. You're going to feel unsteady. It doesn't feel productive, but it's actually the most productive time because everything's happening. And if you have pursued your goal with loving intention, the struggle period is shorter.

However, you can't resist it. You have to embrace it and just let it be. The struggle period is there so you can build up, refresh and reset your energy. This is a great time to read books that nourish your growth mindset so your mind can advance and be ready for the breakthrough. Because when the breakthrough comes, you'll need all the energy to apply it.

So, challenges in the struggle are not there to stop you. Challenges are there to help you grow. Every challenge on the destination towards your intentions, goals, dreams, desires or whatever you want to call it is an opportunity for you to learn something and grow into the next version of yourself.

It's important to only focus on the next step so you don't get overwhelmed, and you can receive the next step. Take one step at a time, but always have the essence of your vision and what you want to achieve in your mind.

I hope you've learned a lot from my chapter, and I just want to share with you that my master gifts are mindfulness, knowing, intention, love, gratitude, forgiveness and belief. As you probably noticed, love is central to those seven master gifts.

The forgiveness one nearly killed me. It was really hard to write because I struggled through it, and I grew so much through it and had so many realisations. But, wow, it was evolutionary because when you get beyond forgiveness, that's where peace is. And peace is a high vibration, where you can access a well of love, a well of anything that you want.

I will leave you with that, and I hope that reading this chapter has ignited something in you.

Please reach out to me on my socials. I am here to help anyone who

Wisdom of Wealth

is awakening and wanting to cross the bridge to awakening their fullest potential.

Too many people are asleep in the world, not realising what's there, waiting for them to claim.

And so, because I've walked the bridge, I'm helping people cross to their awakening. Because once you are awake, you can never fall asleep again. Take care.

About Karen

Hi, I'm Karen.

I'm a multi-award-winning entrepreneur and author and the founder of Serenity Press, MMH Press, KMD Books, and Duchess Serenity Press.

I'm a multi-genre author of over forty books, a Forbes influencer, a three-time TEDx speaker, and a proud mum of six.

I'm an advanced Law of Attraction practitioner who teaches people how to attract anything they want into their lives, and I write about my success principles as K P Weaver.

My annual retreats are sought-after events with featured famous guests and are hosted in an Irish castle.

I'm passionate about sharing my extensive knowledge and vibrant energy with others. I have a 'no excuse' policy because if I can do it, anyone can!

I believe in the power of mums in business, leading the way for the next generation to live to their highest potential.

Wisdom of Wealth

I'm on a mission to share the power of stories with the world.

You can contact me via this link:
https://www.kpwofficial.com/

Kelly Bowen

Seeking Wealth: A Path To Prosperity

There's no easy way to say it … in the cultivation of wealth in my life over the past fifteen years, there have been some big lessons, and each lesson has shaped me into the woman I am today. And that is a woman I deeply love, can trust wholeheartedly, carries herself with grace, feels with her whole heart, consistently shows up and always rises beyond what is in front of her, no matter the circumstances. She is a woman who has created a stable business that gives her a level of true fulfilment, time and money freedom—a business built on the foundation of her heart and authentic self-expression. She serves humanity and helps the collective shift to a new level of consciousness and abundance.

But it wasn't always like this for me. I had to become this woman, which took time, devotion and immense compassion toward me. Trust me when I say I had some pretty great self-sabotaging patterns! I had them by the bucket load!

Wisdom of Wealth

I'm personally a big believer that we learn best through real, authentic stories, and our greatest teacher will always be our lived experience. Since I can't give you my personal lived experience of what I have learned about creating wealth in the last fifteen years, I will give you the next best thing.

I want to share with you the lessons and embodied wisdom I've received through my story and my lived experience, and I hope you have a good laugh along the way because I sure have as I've taken myself down memory lane with you.

Since my journey to wealth has been through creating my own business, or what I like to call My Mission Empire of Light, I will share with you what this has been for me.

If I had to sum it up, I'd steal this common recruitment phrase, which goes something like, One day, you're celebrating with the most fancy champagne you can buy, and the next, you're sitting on razor blades!

Think of the champagne as the wins, the money effortlessly finding its way to your bank account, all the soul-mate clients, the perks of being your own boss babe and everything falling into perfect alignment.

And the razor blades? Well, that's you going through a gazillion ego deaths, dark nights of the soul and just a casual spiritual awakening on a lazy Tuesday afternoon.

So, let's start at the beginning.

This may be the greatest lesson thus far: business is a right of passage. There are no shortcuts, and there's no escaping it.

It's only taken me four failed businesses and a mammoth amount of personal development, soul-searching, the capacity to deal with gut-wrenching uncertainty, evolution, business mentors and a willingness to fail forward over and over again, to accept and embody this truth and become who I needed to create it all.

I very quickly concluded that I could either be entitled and impatient about the process or make peace with the fact that this is the process, get playful with it, have fun with it, and most importantly, learn from it!

Kelly Bowen

I see so many people wanting to get into business, thinking it will magically and rapidly save them from their current broke situation. And I can say this because I sure did! The truth is, business won't ever save you, it will school you, and you certainly cannot create abundance, if you're coming from scarcity!

This is not how the laws of this universe work, as much as I wish it did. The amount of magical thinking I had around this was insane! And I was a sucker for a get rich promise! One of my four failed businesses was a natural health product, promising weight loss and healing your gut of incurable ailments.

They wanted people to invest a $32k cash buy-in for five per cent of the company, promising a return of $100k plus within a couple of years, and the return was guaranteed to continue to grow.

Beauty! I thought. It's just the thing I was looking for. So, I did whatever it took, I got the money together and handed over everything I had!

No sighting or signing of contracts. No looking at market research or product research and no company background checks. Just here you go! Blind faith and a cash deposit. Done!

I can feel you all squirming at my naivety and ignorance, even I am, as I write this. Might I add, this was against the 'good advice' of the friends I did have who were in business, but I was certain this would work, and of course, I knew better. My psychic healer at the time, who was also invested in this company, told me she had a good feeling about it and that I should get in now! This was it, my big shot.

I started putting my heart and soul into selling this product. I had stands at all the health and wellness festivals Australia-wide that year. I was all in! As you can imagine, this failed spectacularly, and I would have done better spending this money on buying lotto tickets.

There went my dream. All my 'life savings' I had poured into the initial investment and *all* the *extra* money I put into travelling around to the festivals.

Wisdom of Wealth

I was stripping at this time of my life. Yes, you read that correctly. I was an exotic dancer, so that was a lot of lap dances I just torched, and my Industry exit plan was shattered.

I was back at ground zero. Bank account $0.

My foolishness shattered my ego and pride, and I was a little jaded by the people in this world because I had just learnt the hard way that you can't take people at face value!

The true make of a person's character and trustworthiness is defined through their consistent actions. When someone shows you who they are, believe them. Words mean nothing unless there is action and follow-through to back it up.

Then there was the obvious lesson.

When it comes to business, get everything in writing. Do your research and maybe don't consult a psychic for wealth advice. Hahaha! And maybe I shouldn't be looking for a 'Get Rich Quick Idea', no matter how seductive it sounds. And maybe I want to start thinking about creating something sustainable with a long-term goal.

So, with all this new wisdom, I decided to have another go at creating wealth for myself. And trust me when I say it takes something to dust yourself off and go again.

This was one of those huge ego-burn moments and the death of a very innocent part of myself. This experience fundamentally changed who I was and how I saw the world.

But luckily, I had a few things going for me.

Resilience: is something my childhood forced me to develop by the truckload.

Youth: I was only twenty-eight.

I had a burning desire to make something of my life and make a difference in the world. And my hustle game was on point.

Reluctantly, I went back to stripping, and it wouldn't take too long to cash up with those lap dances, and I would have the money to go again.

Kelly Bowen

This time, though, I was going to be smarter.
No more falling for the 'Get Rich Quick Promises'.
No More relying on others to make it happen.
I thought, let's go back to what I know.
'Let's build something I have total control over and really enjoy.'
So, I decided to open a personal training business.
I already had my Cert 4 in Fitness, and I thought it shouldn't be too hard.
I'll just lean back on the fact I was a world-champion water skier.

Something I achieved at nineteen and thought I could leverage to give me immediate authority and expert status in the health and fitness space. It made sense to me, as people naturally respect athletes because they know what kind of dedication is required to become the very best at something.

For the next ten years, I was immersed in my training to achieve a world title. I intimately knew how to train the body for peak performance, and I could also add my new nutrition knowledge from that failed health product.

It was genius! It made total logical sense. So, with my new lot of life savings from all those lap dances, I rented a space, brought all the fancy gym equipment, and declared myself 'Open for business!' Alpha Fitness & Wellbeing was born. I was so proud of myself, and I thought this idea was about as foolproof as I would get.

Wrong again!

This time, I learned how to have a successful business. There is so much more to it than just being highly skilled, giving great service, getting awesome results and having a space.

There is this whole other thing called marketing.

This is also around when I started sitting with the question, who do I need to become to create the things I desire?

And, I didn't want to become a marketer. I wanted to be a personal trainer and an athlete again. And I hated marketing! It didn't make sense to me. I didn't enjoy anything about it. I certainly didn't want to share

Wisdom of Wealth

about myself or my life on social media publicly. I didn't want to have to be seen, and definitely not like that.

It felt exposing and attention-seeking.

I was also in deep conflict with myself because by day, I was a health coach who was supposed to be an athlete, and by night, I was a stripper, a first-class party girl who loved a cheeky line with a vodka chaser.

I was living a double life and in total conflict with myself. I wanted it to be easy. I wanted the clients to come to me because I was great at what I did. And, with that level of entitlement, cognitive dissonance, avoidance and fear.

Thank God my lap dance business was going strong and allowed me to keep pouring money into my new money-gobbling venture. Otherwise, it would have been over before it began. Instead of cleaning myself up and learning to market online as my mentors advised, I thought I could bypass it all. I decided it didn't apply to me. So, in my brilliance, I thought, let's learn how to coach. It makes total sense. I love human behaviour.

If I have more skills, I can solve more problems, and I can make way more of a difference in people's lives. Surely, more people will want to work with me now. I'll be a person of high value and make a big difference, right?

Nope. Wrong again!

There were two huge problems I wasn't yet willing to address. One was that I was totally out of alignment with myself. My double life was killing me, and I desperately needed some therapy. In hindsight, I know my soul was leading me to coaching because it was saying she's not getting it. My soul was lovingly sending me somewhere where it knew my curious mind would be captivated, somewhere that would light the problem up in my face like a neon sign so bright that I couldn't miss it.

The other probelm was that I had just fallen into the loop I see so many new coaches fall into. A loop that has their business always staying on the ground. They think they need more skills to succeed because they don't want to learn business. The truth is, if you want to build a successful business, you need to be great at what you do and exceptional at business, too.

My clever, little soul was so right, as ALL this did was wake me up to all my gaps and show me how much inner work I had to do to get to where I wanted to be.

Urgh! So exhausting!

My entitled need for instant gratification was hating this, but did I give up? No, but trust me, I easily could have.

By this point, I had invested $40k into that failed health product, at least $60k into mentors, my personal growth and development, plus another $20k to fit out my studio and space hire, and $6k into a website that wasn't really set up for lead capture and this was all in two years.

At this point, I wasn't making anywhere near enough to cover my basic living costs. I had maxed out my credit cards. I had taken as many personal loans as that bank would give me, and going back to the strip club to make up the difference was becoming unbearable. I was feeling pretty defeated and in total adrenal burnout.

I remember thinking maybe I just wasn't meant for business. I just couldn't get this whole marketing piece figured out.

And I was well into my healing journey, which was my first conscious experience of a dark night of the soul and spiritual awakening rolled into one.

Anyway, as fate would have it, in 2014, my best friend Gaby offered me a part-time role in her finance brokerage. Gaby said, 'Why don't you come and learn finance with me? You can stop stripping and build your business on the side like I have with my coaching business. Worst-case scenario, you will have a solid career that will make you easily employable if you need it.'

I replied with a *hell yes*! I just had to get out of stripping. I didn't care how at this point. I just had to get out. It was killing my mind, body and soul by the end, and I jumped at this opportunity.

Wisdom of Wealth

All the inner work I had been doing had ripped my blinders off, and I could see how unhealthy it was for me to be in that environment, as it didn't support the new person I had become. It was one of those situations where once I saw it, I couldn't un-see it.

Although the path of finance had been the one with the most flow, it sure came with some hard lessons at the beginning, but it has whipped me into shape the most. My first twelve months in finance were a continuous face-off with my inner rebel.

You know the one I spoke about before who was so entitled and didn't want to listen to her mentors and thought the rules didn't apply to her? Yep, she had to die. Or, more affectionately, evolve and stop rebelling against herself and those who were trying to help her.

I was all about doing things my way, and close enough was good enough. In finance, there's just no tolerance for this because finance is all about following a process and accuracy.

In the early days, I used to shake with anxiety every time I submitted a finance application because I feared what it was going to be flagged for. I never realised just how much I was wired to go against the grain of everything. Following a simple process seemed impossible to me. The worst part was I got it intellectually, but I was unconsciously hard-wired to do the opposite.

I literally had to unlearn how I learned and relearn how to do this. No wonder I couldn't make any of my past businesses work. It was excruciating. It felt like I was dying a thousand deaths daily. I sometimes remember crying with frustration that I couldn't get this right for the life of me. But I was devoted.

I was willing to do whatever it took to transform this part of myself and make this work. I could see the pain it was causing in every area of my life, not just in my capacity to build abundance. There was no part of my life this behaviour was not affecting.

And in time, like lots of time, persistence and repetition, my processing got better and better. I learnt how to follow a process and execute a task to full completion without my inner rebel hijacking me and having a field day.

Gaby believed in me. She taught me how to believe in myself again and generously gave me a bucket load of love and much-needed mentoring. This was one of the greatest gifts I have ever received and definitely something I will always be eternally grateful for.

Eventually, an opportunity presented itself where I could become a partner in a finance brokerage firm.

It meant I had to let go of my beloved coaching business. Alpha Fitness & Wellbeing, in that time, had transformed into a small twelve-month mastermind called Exceptional Living, and believe it or not, I had learnt how to become a marketer, and I was finally starting to connect with my soul mate clients.

I had been doing soul work at the time, and my multidimensionality was starting to come online. My soul was telling me to wrap up the coaching business, go full-time finance, and fully commit to this opportunity wholeheartedly. Even though it made no sense at the time, I wrapped up the coaching business and went all in with finance.

This is where I learned to trust and surrender to my soul's guidance because she knows best, and what she has planned for me, when I listened, was even more delicious than I could have imagined in my limited human consciousness.

Fast forward another year, and I had the opportunity to buy the brokerage in its entirety, and I jumped at it. Not only was there this opportunity, but the brokerage was starting to transform into a vehicle to make a real difference in the world and help leaders in the coaching space amplify their messages, which made my heart sing.

We realised we could use personal loan finance to finance coaching packages and programs. This meant I had an opportunity to make the education people so desperately need more affordable and accessible than ever before and solve three of the biggest challenges coaching businesses face.

1. Client affordability and accessibility can be achieved because with finance a $20k product becomes around $100 a week to a client.
2. Cash flow—because with finance, the coach gets paid in full from day one with no risk to their business.
3. The management of payment plans—this is all outsourced to the finance company.

This excited me so much, and the potential ripple effect it has to shift the collective consciousness is massive.

Five years later, Lifestyle Finance Aus now supports hundreds of epic leaders and game changers worldwide by backing their coaching packages with finance. We fund millions of dollars into this space every year.

When my soul gave me the nudge to go all in with finance, I had no idea this was where it was headed or that it was even possible. This experience has really shown me it's not always about finding your purpose or passion. It's about finding purpose and passion in what you do, and abundance will come.

I wasn't looking for finance, but it found me.

I just wanted to get out of stripping, and my deeper desire to make a difference and live a life of true purpose, freedom and abundance is what I believe transformed this opportunity into what it became.

This brings me to my last major lesson in creating wealth.

Allowing myself to take this journey got me to a level of abundance that was well beyond my wildest dreams as a little girl, as I don't come from wealth, and my parents were not business people.

At this point in my story, I was already living a life I could only have dreamed of, yet when I was honest with myself, I still had two big pieces missing. I had built a business that was solely reliant upon me. This meant that when I worked, I made lots of money, but when I didn't work, I didn't get paid. I was a great solopreneur and had created a very rewarding job for myself, but I didn't have the true freedom I desired. Also, I was still chasing the next big thing. I thought that when I got there, I would be happy. I would be enough. I would be loveable, and I could finally rest. But, when I got there, there was always another there. It would always leave me with momentary satisfaction but no long-term fulfilment. I was numb and chasing the next big thing to make me feel alive.

What came next was a blind-siding dark night of the soul and yet another spiritual awakening. AKA the most powerful life lesson I have ever experienced.

This is the one that had me shift into real freedom, true fulfilment and abundance.

This final piece grounded me into the woman I mentioned in the opening sentences: a business owner who feels deeply, carries herself with grace, and is a trustworthy leader.

I wish I started with this piece because it would have made the journey so much more graceful, yet far less entertaining, because everything up to this point was symptomatic of this final piece.

And that's nervous system regulation.

Unbeknown to me, I had been living in such a chronic state of nervous system dysregulation, driven by my crazy, over-achieving, hyper-independent, people-pleasing, workaholic persona, which I had perfected to avoid feeling at all costs.

My entire system was shot and hard-wired for chaos. This meant the more I tried to create stability in my life, the more this would throw my whole system into mayhem because it was so unfamiliar to it.

Stability and time freedom meant I would get to rest, and if I got to rest, I would have to feel. And what was in that feeling box was some thirty-seven years of suppressed childhood trauma that I would rather subconsciously die than feel. Stability and freedom, ironically, were terrifying and deeply

Wisdom of Wealth

unsafe for my nervous system. So, instead of feeling, I used to create a dichotomy of experiences, where I would experience extreme highs and lows simultaneously. Even though I had gotten this far in the abundance game, it was a battle. It was like constantly taking two steps forward and one step back. I would get ahead financially and then manifest something totally random, like my cat getting hit by a car, and to save her life, it would cost exactly my savings.

I was falling deeply in love with someone, and at the same time, I was falling out with my best friend, and we didn't talk for six months. There was even one time when I had significant business growth and then had that whole month's income stolen from me. This left me with nothing, and I still had to find a way to pay staff.

This is where I learnt the real truth about manifestation, and I wish more people were talking about it, especially in the money and business space.

The Truth is, our nervous system will only allow you to expand to and hold the level of abundance and freedom you feel safe with.

Until you learn to feel safe with large sums of abundance and time freedom, your bank account will always find its way back to its default mode, and your time grid will get filled to capacity, so it always feels like you have none!

When it comes to manifestation and creating the life we deeply desire and feeling it fully, we don't get what we want. We get who we are somatically. Because we live in a vibrational, relational universe, which means we cannot create what we are not.

Put simply, it was impossible for me to create consistent and expanding realities of abundance, love, fulfilment, peace, joy, fun, pleasure and play because, at my very core, I had not yet cultivated this.

I was vibrationally putting out to the universe chaos, chaos, chaos, and that's exactly what I got. So, I had to let it all in. I had to feel those feelings I had been running from all my life.

Yep, the same ones I would rather die than feel, to release all that trapped energy in my body and return to the truth of who I am. It was this trapped energy that was causing the chaos. My unwillingness to feel these feelings is why I felt numb and why I always chased the next big thing.

Feeling! This changed my internal thermostat from surviving to thriving; by far, it was the bravest and most courageous thing I have ever done.

I remember the very moment I decided to do this. I was struggling with it so much, and one of my besties, Carissa, who was sitting with me at the time, asked, 'What would happen if you let the emotional dam wall break?'

I was shocked and asked her, 'Have you ever seen a dam wall break? They usually flood the town, and everyone drowns!'

Carissa said softly, 'You don't have to let it out like that.'

I was confused and had a look on my face that said, do you not know me at all? 'I don't see how it can happen any other way.'

The dam wall broke, and I can happily report that no one died or drowned, even though there were some touch-and-go moments. The flood and intensity of emotions I had to feel and clean up were enormous.

Was this a fun or an easy project? No.

It was huge and is still a constant commitment to myself daily to let my feelings in and no longer self-betray or self-abandon.

It was lifesaving!

Learning to feel and be vulnerable and re-parent my inner child has been by far the most rewarding thing I have ever done. To have peace and truly feel safe in my body and have my realities reflect this is priceless. The only thing I wish for is that someone told me about the magic of nervous system regulation much sooner. This was the piece that felt like it plugged my soul into my body, and my whole life lit up in the most glorious and fabulous colours.

So, with that in mind, I'll leave you with these final thoughts on what I believe it takes to create success and abundance as an entrepreneur.

If someone as clueless and naive in the world of business as I was, who

Wisdom of Wealth

continuously failed forward so spectacularly, can make it this far, so can anyone else. The mistakes and ups and downs are part of it. You'll get there if you keep going. If something doesn't work, dust yourself off and try again. Follow your nudges. It's your soul trying to say this way.

Be devoted to the journey and your evolution. It's key.

Commit to your dream with every aspect of your being with unwavering certainty.

And remember, the only thing that kills the spirit is staying down. Despite what your pride might say, your soul always has it in the tank to go again. It only wants the best for you.

We live in an abundant universe. Scarcity is a mind construct that can be dismantled.

I believe in you!

You're worth it!

You got this!

About Kelly

My name is Kelly Bowen, and I'm a New Earth Leader and the founder of The Heaven Within Foundation, The Lifestyle Show Podcast, CEO of Lifestyle Finance Australia and co-host of the Inspired Conversations on the Em and Kel Podcast. I'm a speaker, Quantum Coach, 5D Business, Ascension and Abundance Mentor.

With over twelve years immersed in finance, personal growth, spiritual and business evolution, I'm deeply passionate about seeing every soul on this planet living fully from passion, purpose and abundance as a birthright.

Contact via the links below:
http://www.lifestylefinanceco.com
http://https://www.inspiredconversationspodcast.com
https://www.heavenwithinfoundation.org/

Kim Kent

Money Matters

I feel my whole life has revolved around money. My go-to memories when I think back on my childhood, involve never having enough, parents who fought over money, hearing about how Dad never paid enough child support and how hard life was.

I associated money with struggle. I dreamed of being rich, but I thought that was a dream for greedy people. I chased the dollar, doing extra chores around the house for extra pocket money, but my savings game was not very strong. From the moment I could legally work, I got my first job. I hustled, made money weekly, and turned eighteen still with zero money in the bank. I definitely knew how to spend much better than save.

I was constantly stressed. I always felt like there was never enough. I always got a late fee on my phone bill because I never paid it on time.

I was never truly without money. I worked hard. I paid my bills and had a social life. However, I constantly spent my money before I earned it, and I definitely embodied the 'broke uni student' identity well.

Kim Kent

As I finished university, my ambition was raging. I was so determined to be successful and wealthy because I saw my parents sacrifice a level of freedom and happiness for a stable income, and in my heart, I knew I needed both. I wanted children one day, and I wanted to show them that you can have your cake and eat it, too. I didn't know how I was going to do it, but I did know that I had to be the one to break the cycle of scarcity and lack in our family.

A few years into my adult life, my entire world and perspective on money changed. I was twenty-seven and had built an incredibly successful online multi-level marketing (MLM) business that was paying me thousands of dollars a month, residually. I was earning more money than I ever thought possible for this online business. I worked my own hours and as my own boss. However, I still felt broke. I still felt like there wasn't enough and that I couldn't get ahead.

I attended a weekend seminar about money mindset, and I learned about universal laws, self-worth and how to manage my money following specific principles. I was like a sponge for this information. It was like the light bulbs finally went off in my mind. The switch had finally flicked on.

And so began a life-changing journey and a true marker of change toward my self-worth and my relationship with money. This seminar was the stepping stone of my journey to creating my path to financial freedom.

Because of this work and the healing I did, I now know so deeply that my life's purpose is, and has always been, helping women just like me to break the generational 'hand-me-down' of a scarcity mentality.

I'm now thirty-two, and I've spent years learning and implementing what many well-known money coaches preach in their books and courses. I have tweaked the strategy to align with the ambitious, action-taking woman, and the feedback from my clients always comes back with how I make making money feel fun. Wrapped in a feminine energy vibe, I always hold the safest space for them to share their financial circumstances unapologetically.

Wisdom of Wealth

I am really excited to share as much as I can in this short chapter. I focus on the 3 Pillars for building wealth when working with my clients.

1. Mindset
2. Manifestation
3. Management.

Mindset

You were born into this world as a blank canvas. Pure energy and an empty mind. Then, your most influential carers—most commonly your parents—teach you what life is about based on their own perceptions of what's right and wrong. Including how to think, feel and behave with money. So, yes, feel free to blame those lovely parents of yours for all that stress, frustration and lack.

But my advice is, as much as you can thank your parents for f*cking up your relationship with money, it's one hundred per cent up to you to take ownership and responsibility to move forward, heal the childhood wounds, and create the relationship with money that you truly desire.

If you experienced any scarcity or lack around money growing up, either from what you heard your parental figures say, or how you saw them behave with money, you carry that scarcity with you now. You have experienced a level of trauma that just needs to be healed.

Your subconscious beliefs run the show right now. If you truly spend time looking back on your childhood, think of a memory where a poor money story played out and recalibrate the truth. You will begin to rewire your subconscious mind, change your own money stories, and change the way you attract, save and spend money moving forward.

I used to constantly hear things such like, 'Money doesn't grow on trees … rich people are greedy … we can't afford it … you have to work really damn hard for money.' Does any of this sound familiar?

These stories ran the show in my mind, so no wonder I hit burnout in my business many times and never felt like I had enough. And no wonder I spent my income before it landed in my account because I never wanted to be viewed as a greedy person.

If you can get extremely clear on all the money stories you heard as a child and what you might still be saying or hearing today, then that's the first step.

Then, you need to go to a time in your past when you remember one of those stories playing out. Take yourself out of the situation and get clear on the real truth.

Was it that your mum was a single parent? Did she have children early and couldn't finish her studies? Did that mean she could only get a minimum wage job, and she never wanted her children to feel like she couldn't provide? So, when you asked for something, and you heard, 'Money doesn't grow on trees,' maybe it was because your mum didn't want you to think it was her who limited your desires. Maybe it was easier to blame the bigger picture or the universe. Maybe she was stressed and felt like she wasn't doing a good job as a mum. Maybe the real truth was she was scared, felt unstable, and she didn't know if she could pay next week's rent. But she was a fierce and unconditionally loving mother who never wanted her kids to worry or see her in pain.

When you begin to get really clear on the actual truth, you start to heal. You begin to love at a higher level, raise your awareness and think from a wealthier consciousness.

So, what was really going on at home when you were a child? Can you find the love and the gift in any scarcity you have experienced?

Manifestation

When I first heard it, this word was definitely filed away in the woo-woo section—being a girl who was so scientific, all about facts, case studies and viewing anything spiritual as the 'hippy' way of life. I was such a

Wisdom of Wealth

logical thinker and so disconnected from my spiritual side that whenever I heard people talk about manifestation, I rolled my eyes.

As I matured and started investing in personal development, I learned about quantum physics and how the world is made up of energy. The way they explained it was like my logical brain was having an orgasm. I frothed over this information, and suddenly, it was like everything in the world made sense. This topic is a whole book in itself. So, I will keep this short and sweet and aligned with money.

If everything is made up of energy, then I am just energy, you are just energy, and money is just energy. Money is just a measurable form of energy, and we live in a time when there is less physical cash and money is numbers on a screen that travels through a frequency between technology. Literal energy frequencies.

Money responds to our energetic vibration—our ability to hold space for it. Our emotions about money are what dictate our relationship with it. Therefore, if you stay feeling and behaving in a state of scarcity, this will affect your ability to attract, receive and spend it. If your emotions are synchronised with abundance, your ability to attract, receive and spend will look completely different.

I want you to know that I'm no manifestation guru, and there is a lot to learn about. What I learned, experienced first-hand, and now teach my clients is that if you want to manifest more money, you must be the vibrational match. This means how you behave with money. Your emotions, conscious and unconscious, trigger your behaviour.

Mindset plays a huge role in manifestation, but you can't just think more money into your world. You must feel it, and you must act in accordance with that wealthier version of yourself.

You see, we are constantly manifesting. Everything in your life right now, you manifested. Your current financial position and your current relationship with money, you manifested. So, you have the power to change what you manifest.

It's time to get really clear on your money habits. Are you emotionally reactive with money? What is your spending behaviour? Are you handing over your power to money and allowing money to dominate the relationship and influence your feelings? Or can you say you are one hundred per cent operating in your personal power with money?

The more you can put your ego aside and get really vulnerable and clear with your money behaviours, the more you can start adjusting them and practising the rituals of a wealthy person. I love teaching my clients this work. There is no cookie-cutter approach either. It is empowering to know that we get to create the rituals and the behaviours that make us feel wealthy and support us in attuning to deep trust, stability, opportunity and receivership.

Management

Yes, I agree that reading the term "management" is undoing all the sexy, fun vibes I intend to exude when I teach about money. This word might trigger some not-so-nice memories of a shitty job you had, or it might make that little girl or boy inside you want to throw a tantrum because they don't want to be responsible yet.

But let's bring some lightness and fun to this word. In my world, money management equals freedom. Management requires structure, and with structure, you create freedom. You begin to embrace your personal power, take your control back and align with the *Universal Law of Handling What You Have*. This is my favourite universal law, and can completely change how you think, feel and behave with money.

The more you learn to handle what you have, the more you're telling the universe that you are ready to have more. If you don't learn to control your money, you will lose what you have until it's at a capacity you can handle.

Have you ever heard about the person who won the Lotto, and twelve months later, they're more broke than before? They didn't know how to handle $1m and enjoyed it back down to the capacity they could manage.

Wisdom of Wealth

Now, I could write a whole book just on this universal law itself, but this is not that book, so here are some tips to get you started with making this universal law work for you.

If money is just energy, and if energy loves to flow, and if flow loves organisation, then money will flow to where it is most organised. Here lies your best piece of advice to get more money flowing to you. It's time to organise your money.

So, let's reprogram how you think about money management and see it as the ultimate opportunity to create a more sexy, fun flow with your finances. I make this effortless when I teach my clients my Signature Money Blueprint.

I teach my clients how to handle what they have by getting more organised and creating a structure with how they budget. By doing this, they no longer feel restricted. They'll always have more than enough flowing through their accounts for all their lifestyle costs. And finally, feel that sense of freedom with their money.

It sounds simple, and it is. You can follow a simple step-by-step process to start handling what you have. However, you probably wouldn't be reading this book if it was easy.

You've been managing and handling your money a certain way for a long time now. It's your comfort zone, and you keep reassuring yourself that you're doing a good job, even though you keep spending more than you earn You're relying on a credit card, or you keep justifying why you're dipping into your savings when what you really want is a juicy buffer in the bank and to have enough money for a deposit on your dream house or whatever that money goal is for you.

Here are the steps:

- Remove all delusions around money and audit your last twelve months of spending.
- Get crystal clear on your spending and saving categories.

Kim Kent

- Project your next twelve months of income and spending.
- Clear up any money leaks and set realistic savings and spending goals.

Put all data into my Signature Money Blueprint spreadsheet that is pre-formulated to organise your money into percentages.

Allocate your money following universal law and money energetics to support your personal power and money manifestations, so you never have to worry about money again.

And voilà! This actually makes money fun, you feel empowered AF, and you actually start attracting opportunities to earn more and save more.

My husband and I attracted $45k from this process.

Our new property build kept getting delayed for random reasons, and at first, it was annoying, as you can imagine. Then COVID-19 hit us in early 2020, and the government released grants to new home buyers and builders. We were eligible for the grant even though the grant was created to encourage people to buy or build. Since we're already on our way, we received this money and used it as a deposit. Alas, an extra $45k into our wealth-building account.

You attract more money when you manage your money more frequently and align with universal law. It comes in ways, shapes and forms you'd never expect, but you feel more abundant than ever. You should take one step at a time, clean up your money and upgrade your level of organisation.

If you want to access my Signature Money Blueprint, where I provide you with a step-by-step process and the support and accountability to implement it so you can clean up your money, get out of debt, stop spending more than you earn and start creating your path to financial freedom, then join me and hundreds of other women taking their money power back inside my Wealthy As F*ck Money Program.

You can apply at https://kimkent.mykajabi.com/wealthyasfuck

In Conclusion

There's so much I desire to keep sharing with you: the intimate money details, the challenges and triumphs, the systems and protocols. There is an abundance of knowledge and skills to pass on. It can seem overwhelming because it's an overload of new information trying to push out the old money stories and conditioned beliefs from your childhood and way of life.

I get it. It can be a lot.

But you know what else is a lot? Living with anxiety, worry, concern, fear and around money, and not having enough. I know you don't want a life full of lack and struggle. I know you have dreams that require cash.

Please do yourself, your future self, your children, and the generations to come a huge favour. Decide that enough is enough, and you're committing to doing the work to learn the skills, upgrade your mindset and break the 'hand-me-down' shitty money beliefs. The grass truly is green on the other side. It is lush, green, and liberating when you break through to self-sabotaging thoughts, feelings and behaviours with your money.

I cannot wait to see the steps you take and the choices you make to support your wealth creation.

Please feel invited to connect with me on social media, consume all my free content and even work with me to fast-track your results.

You are ready.

It is your time.

About Kim

Hi, my name is Kim Kent, and I'm a Money Coach, Money Mindset and Management Specialist, Keynote Speaker and the creator of Signature Money Blueprint. I help hundreds of women inside my program to never worry about money again.

I help ambitious businesswomen break through their money mindset blocks, heal any trauma around money and learn to manage their money using universal law to get out of debt, stop spending more than they earn and start creating their path to financial freedom.

With over ten years as an entrepreneur, I've built seven-figure online businesses and impacted thousands of women's lives with my coaching and support.

In 2020, I was in Yahoo Finances' top six Mindset and Business Coaches. I'm all about getting my clients the results they need and fast. I'm extremely dedicated to my work.

Wisdom of Wealth

I'm also a new mumma, a wine lover, and you will always find me chasing the beach and tropical destinations.

Contact me and apply for my program at:

Instagram handle @kimkent__

https://kimkent.mykajabi.com/wealthyasfuck

Laura Elizabeth

Mindful Money In Your Sleep

In today's fast-paced world, time is a precious commodity. Many people find themselves caught in a never-ending cycle of work, leaving them with little time for their personal lives, hobbies, or relaxation. However, there is a powerful concept that allows you to regain control over your time while still increasing your income—passive income streams that make you money in your sleep.

What if I told you that you could achieve this goal by leveraging the principles of mindfulness, abundance mindset, and the Law of Attraction?

In the following pages, I will break it down into actionable steps so you can make money in your sleep.

Read on to unleash your financial sovereignty.

The Power of Mindfulness

Mindfulness is the practice of being fully present in the moment without judgement. It is a state of focused awareness that can help you make better decisions, reduce stress, and increase your overall well-being.

Wealth can be a reflection of implementing mindful choices in your life to succeed. Success begins with well-structured planning. Instead of rushing through your to-do list, take a moment to breathe and focus on your priorities. Consider setting aside specific blocks of time for different tasks, and then commit your full attention to each one when its time arrives. This mindful approach to planning allows you to make the most of your day without feeling scattered.

Effective communication is vital in business. Mindful listening, where you fully engage with what others are saying, fosters better relationships and understanding. Repeating what has been noted for clarity or asking appropriate questions for efficiency can save time. Time equals money.

Recognising that you can't do everything yourself is a sign of a mindful entrepreneur. Delegating tasks to trusted family or team members lightens your load and empowers those around you, increasing productivity. Many hands make light work!

Remember not to underestimate the power of brief mindfulness breaks throughout the day. Take a few minutes to focus on your breath, relax your body, and clear your mind. These moments of rejuvenation can boost your energy and creativity. In our highly digital age, being mindful of technology is crucial. Set boundaries on when and how you use technology to prevent it from becoming a distraction. Boundaries also help in maintaining a healthy work-life balance.

Consider making a list of what you want to prioritise in your daily life and within your work hours. How would you like to feel? What tasks bring you a sense of purpose and achievement? Focus on these and watch how productive you can be.

What is an Abundance Mindset?

An abundance mindset is the belief that limitless opportunities and resources are available to you. It's a shift from scarcity thinking to a mindset of abundance.

One of the primary reasons people struggle financially is due to a scarcity mindset. This mindset is rooted in fear, doubt, and the belief that there's not enough to go around or that their abilities are not enough (self-doubt) to succeed. It can lead to poor financial decisions and self-sabotaging behaviours.

To cultivate an abundance mindset, one must consciously shift one's beliefs. This process involves recognising negative thought patterns and replacing them with positive, empowering beliefs. Challenge your limiting beliefs about money and wealth and trust that you have the power to change your financial reality.

I learned an incredible process from my mentor, Emma Romano, called Timeline Reset. This process gets to the core of your limiting beliefs. It helps to reframe the neural pathways without going into the story or trauma of past experiences. I revisit this process for myself often and use it with almost every client to assist in shifting the old stagnant beliefs holding them back.

Using the Law of Attraction to Manifest Abundance

The core idea behind the law of attraction is that like attracts like. It suggests that the energy you emit, both consciously and unconsciously, draws corresponding experiences, people and opportunities into your life. When it comes to manifesting abundance, the law of attraction asserts that by maintaining a positive and abundant mindset, you'll naturally attract wealth, prosperity, and opportunities.

To put the Law of Attraction and mindfulness into action, here are some practical steps:

Set Clear Goals

Define your financial objectives with clarity. The more specific and measurable they are, the easier it is to focus your thoughts and energy on them.

Visualise Your Success

Regularly engage in visualisation exercises where you vividly imagine yourself achieving your financial goals, but more importantly, visualise how it makes you feel. If you were financially successful, how would you be feeling? What would your relationships look like? How would you be helping your community? What would your free time look like? By doing this, you reinforce a positive mindset.

Affirmations

Use positive affirmations to reprogram your subconscious mind. Repeatedly affirming your financial success can help eliminate self-doubt and negativity. Always use positive language, the subconscious will only pick up on affirmative language and repeat it multiple times daily for at least thirty days. It is scientifically proven to take thirty days to break a habit.

Examples of positive financial affirmations include:

- I willingly accept money into my life with ease.
- I deserve to receive financial wealth and prosperity.
- I openly receive from many streams of income daily.

Take Inspired Action

While the law of attraction is powerful, taking action toward your goals is essential. Opportunities often arise when you're actively pursuing them. After clearly writing your goals, commit to at least one action towards that goal each day. These could be actions that take thirty seconds, like affirmations, or actions that take thirty minutes, like bookkeeping.

Practice Mindfulness

Incorporate mindfulness techniques into your daily routine, such as meditation and deep breathing. These techniques will help you stay present and focused on your intentions. There is an old Zen saying: 'You should sit in meditation for twenty minutes a day. Unless you're too busy, then you should sit for an hour.'

Multiple Income Streams

In today's dynamic world, the idea of relying on a single income source has become increasingly risky. As a thirty-something entrepreneur and solo mother of three, I understand the importance of diversifying income to achieve financial security and abundance. Multiple income streams can be a game-changer in your quest to attract money in passive ways.

Passive income refers to earnings that don't require constant active involvement. It can come from various sources, such as investments, rental properties, or online businesses.

Just about anything can be monetised these days! As you continue your entrepreneurial journey, creating multiple passive income streams can provide you with financial stability and flexibility.

Consider digital products like eBooks and recorded meditations that can be created once and sold many times over as an easy way to build organic clients and generate passive global income in your sleep. Automation plays a significant role in generating this type of passive income. It involves using technology and systems to streamline and optimise your business operations. This can include email marketing, social media scheduling, or even setting up e-commerce stores that run themselves.

By combining the principles of mindfulness, an abundance mindset and the Law of Attraction with innovative financial strategies, you can take back your time and make money while you sleep.

This guide has provided you with a step-by-step road map to achieve this goal. Remember that it takes dedication, patience and continuous

Wisdom of Wealth

self-improvement to succeed on your journey toward financial abundance and time freedom.

Start today with small actionable steps and watch as your life transforms into one of abundance and fulfilment.

About Laura

Hi, I'm Laura Elizabeth, a trailblazing change-maker and advocate for women's empowerment, author of nine bestselling titles, director at Maven Press, *creatress* of Kuntea and owner of Laura Elizabeth Wellness.

I am dedicated to creating intimate experiences for conscious women ready to step into a deeper layer of understanding of themselves. I assist them in embracing and embodying their sensuality, reclaiming their voices and owning their personal power.

I offer womb and yoni massage therapy, reiki attunements and a catalogue of workshops, education and training events online and in person, focusing on women's health.

I am also the woman behind a steadfast, hand-crafted organic product range, topping its tenth year, including the risqué yoni steaming brand Kuntea for reproductive health and wellness.

My love of writing and being a keeper of women's stories has led me most recently to create Maven Press Publishing. I am delighted to doula storytellers through the conception, gestation and birth of their books into the world as they step deeper into their truth as change-makers.

A naturally gifted psychic medium born on the East Coast of Fife, Scotland, I immigrated to Perth, Western Australia, as a pre-teen in 1999. With two decades of experience cultivating my skills as an energy worker and holding space for clients, I offer the safest and most profoundly intimate containers for women to encounter deep transformation.

A boundary pusher and taboo smasher, I am best known for my real, quirky and honest guidance, ensuring the deepest empathy and understanding without judgement. I believe keeping a healthy sense of humour is important to stay grounded and authentic.

My service to clients is most definitely a niche. Yet, I believe it is the real missing link in human connection and healing for women. We are programmed to think, feel, and act based on the needs of others. But we unleash our real magic when we set aside time to explore honouring, nurturing, and loving ourselves back into a belief of radical acceptance and remembering our magnificence.

A passionate solo mother of three, leading by example, smashing goals, and living with purpose, I hope to positively influence my own children to reach their full potential and inspire others to do the same.

I hold your hand and love you while you remember how to love yourself.

Contact me at:
Facebook: facebook.com/the_lauraelizabeth
Instagram: instagram.com/the_lauraelizabeth
Website: www.mavenpress.com.au

Lezly Kaye

The Money Matrix

I am Lezly Kaye, a strategic advisor, executive coach, single mother and multimillion-dollar entrepreneur. I have scaled businesses to $60m and $15m in turnover in mere months.

I went from wildly wealthy and emotionally bankrupt to nearly bankrupt and emotionally abundant, to creating a life with it all: wealth, health and freedom. I have traversed the depths of my soul to bring myself into alignment in all areas of my life. Then, I studied the modalities that saw me transform my life in order to embody them. This allowed me to bring medicine to more women and beings who needed the path to prosperity illuminated for them.

In these paragraphs, I hope to inspire, enlighten and encourage those seeking permission to harness the power of belief in their world, go after big things and have the courage to claim everything they desire. To courageously step forward and allow themselves to realise their purpose on this earth is shamelessly to create the life of their dreams in all areas without compromise. We truly live in an abundant existence, and the more people who claim wealth, health, freedom and love in all areas, the more illuminated the path becomes for everyone else.

What are the Secrets to Coding the Money Matrix?

The largest secret to coding the money matrix is that the matrix is actually here to support us. Given that words are spells in spiritual or conscious communities, there's often this term or statement that we need to disengage from the matrix and move away. But the secret is that the matrix is what sustains life. Actually, the matrix is what feeds into the energetic frequency of our souls. So, if you declare that you want to disengage or disconnect, you're actually disconnecting from the game of life. However, the way to win at this game, the money game specifically, is to engage, create change, and show up in the world how you want to see change created. To find people who have cheat codes for the exact things you want to evolve in. People who have learned how to hack the matrix and play the game really truly believe that we are fully supported in seen and unseen ways. When we can believe in possibility and believe that we can have everything we truly desire, then start bringing this belief into fruition through our actions, words and beliefs, then our lives change in big ways.

Suppose you look at money as love. If you look at it as the frequency of love, for example. Our ability to receive love greatly impacts our ability to receive money, and the reason I relate or link money to love is if I love myself deeply, which I do, wouldn't I want financial freedom? Freedom to take myself to mystical places and on enchanting experiences. Wouldn't I only fly business class so I arrive well rested, with a calm nervous system and an ability to use my time effectively? If I loved myself, wouldn't I only eat organic? Wouldn't I only drink the purest water? Wouldn't I have all of this bio-hack equipment like Heelys and Kangin? Wouldn't I only use the best chemical-free cleaning products and only buy sustainable fashion? And all of the other things that aid the quality of our life and the things that we consume that cost money because that is the energetic frequency of our reality.

So when we realise that we are in this game of loving ourselves so deeply that we need to receive love in all ways, including the prosperity and abundance around us, then we can truly open ourselves to receiving the keys to life. One of the biggest keys to our existence and our existence with full ease and grace is actually accepting that prosperity is here to aid us in our evolution to a beautiful, easeful existence within this realm.

Weaving Worlds of Entrepreneurship and Spirituality

First, spirituality is just the relationship and understanding you have with yourself and the world around you. Don't get caught up in labelling yourself in a certain way. If you're using it to mask yourself in a certain way, the key to leaning into our ability to weave worlds is to allow the integration of its ability to just be a way of being in connection to self. And that spirituality and entrepreneurship, this esoteric entrepreneur era that I feel we're coming into as a collective, is exciting and challenging and can change how we do business and operate as a civilisation.

I would especially encourage women in this field to allow themselves to come into balance and union and really focus on their Alpha and Omega qualities, our masculine and feminine, yin and yang. As women, we often get swept up in the very prominent field of only receiving in business. There is this false promise of opening ourselves up to receive then everything will flow. And while that is a requirement, we need to be in energetic alignment and internal balance, a dance if you like. We do need to have alignment in our lives to receive and flow and bring online all that is waiting for us.

However, there is a deeper requirement to be in relationship with our masculine and, more specifically, our inner masculine as women. There is a requirement to understand that our ability to birth and steward big businesses that crack the prosperity code in big ways deeply relies on our ability to integrate our masculine. To have a masculine container of structure, direction and logic in order to allow this uprising of matriarchal businesses. The goal is to have more than matriarchal businesses. It's to have businesses built on the union of both men and women at the helm. To have both our Alpha and Omega energies in a beautiful dance and beautiful weaving of giving and receiving force and flow.

Strategies that Led to my Entrepreneurial Success

For most of my life, an undercurrent of determination always drove me to never give up. I would say that is the biggest key to success and continued success is to not see mistakes as failures or wrong turns as something that will take us to a dead end. There is always another day, there is always another option, and there is always a way through even the darkest moments of our soul.

When I sent one of my companies into administration, it led me to the dark night of the soul and some of the most profound healing journeys I've ever embarked on. It sort of brought me to a crossroads in my life and allowed me to view the world through a whole new lens and really start to witness that.

The big cosmic joke is we're not in control of anything, but we are in control of everything. Because we can control the way we show up in the world. We can control how we react to the world, and once we build a relationship with ourselves and our nervous system, we can show up in the world more aligned with the truth of who we are.

I feel this level of understanding of ourselves that can be bought through adversity can become the building blocks to our next evolution, our next level of success and our next breakthrough into new levels of belief and ability. We can then show up in the world in even bigger ways.

This way of looking at the world led me to birth the next evolution in my return to corporate conciseness, and my program, The Self Responsibility Code, was born—the blueprint for my strategy of living a life in alignment and sustained personal and professional growth. Through harnessing my moments of deep and often confronting lessons, I reflected on the level of radical responsibility it takes to create not only individual transformation but organisational transformation for sustained growth and well-being within the world, specifically in corporate environments.

How to Know When You're in Alignment with Purpose

This is an interesting question because it takes me back to the beginning of my journey, where I didn't actually feel in alignment, but I couldn't quantify the notion. I couldn't put into words what I was feeling or express that lack in any way. I just felt very disconnected from life and my business. I felt sort of in this place of knowing I was here for something but not really feeling connected to what I had created.

I was very new to being in relationship with myself at that point, and I sort of understood that I was feeling disconnected, but I didn't have any other way to process or understand those emotions. I don't even think I fully felt emotions at this point, and I had been emotionally locked down for most of my life.

Fast forward to now, and I think the best way or the easiest way to identify if you are in alignment is it doesn't really feel like work or effort. You get into this place where you're so embodied in who you are and how you show up in the world that you can truly drop into flow states more consistently. It feels less monotonous to complete tasks and joyful to work long hours or be in *intuitive excretion*, as I call it.

There's almost this sense of urgency because you know that the world needs to hear your medicine, but there is a deep balance in how much you work or how many hours you contribute to being on mission because living life is also the mission.

We are here to succeed and thrive in big ways. I think that is when you

Wisdom of Wealth

land in a place of deep alignment where there's no separation from life and living and being on purpose and path. I'm writing this section of the book from the jungles of Costa Rica, and this is my fourth overseas trip in the first six months of the year. People often ask me how I can afford a holiday so often. They often ask if I take a lot of breaks.

The truth is, I don't actually holiday. This is a lifestyle for me. I have intentionally built a life by design where I'm aligned in my work. I'm aligned in the ways I show up in the world. For me, this means truly designing a life that feels the most abundant, alive and prosperous. This level of integration into life allows us to enter the most symbiotic relationships with how we show up in the world. In addition, how abundance and prosperity show up when you're in alignment really just plays into this theme of not having to holiday from your life of building a life of design. For me, it is about aligning with the frequency of the person I am becoming, truly embodying the highest version of me. For instance, I frequently fly business class all around the world.

Even in the beginning stages of building this new iteration of business, this new iteration of myself and the medicine I'm here to deliver in the world, money would always show up. I would commit $20k to travel and not just for travel's sake but in alignment. It would be to see sacred sites, be in medicine ceremonies, or attend training. If I booked these trips in full alignment with my purpose and my soul's work, the money I spent would instantly show up in sales.

Being in relationship with life and myself in big ways allows me to trust in the flow of reciprocity and trust that the earth is deeply holding me. One thing I know is true is that wealth is abundant. There is limitless prosperity, and truly, the intent of this universe is not for us to be in lack.

There is an abundance of resources for us to share, and once we realise resources are abundant and we can tap into that frequency, we just have to remain in faith that we are always looked after. And, in fact, the more we look after ourselves, the more we're looked after in return.

Blocking Your Receiving of Abundance and Prosperity

This one refers to doing the work, doing the deep healing work, understanding our internal landscapes and wounds and excavating those shadows.

I've touched on it in parts of this chapter. There have been moments of deep reflection, dark nights of the soul and deep shadow work, and if we don't do the work to coincide with our success, we lose it all. In fact, this is why I lost it all. At one point, I sent a business into administration for millions of dollars. Even though it was rather successful, I grew the business with ego, and our cash flow just couldn't keep up with the egoic choices I was making.

As grateful as I am for those lessons, I definitely feel like it could have been avoided if I had been in better relationship with myself. If I had, then my motivations for the decisions I made and my understanding of the wounding that caused me not to trust life or myself and seek answers outside of myself. So, ultimately, we can stop ourselves from receiving and actually blow up our lives in big ways if our nervous system can't hold the expansion of wealth, love, and freedom that we call into our lives.

The neuroscience, or more traditionally, how we block ourselves is through limiting beliefs. So, if we don't look at the belief systems that frame our lives and the relationships with our parents, ourselves and our inner child, we can start to undo all the work we've done to create success. It's not until we deeply understand ourselves that we can create in more aligned and sustainable ways, ensuring we maintain the expansion we desire.

Why am I Here and What legacy Will I Leave?

I'm here to weave worlds between spirituality and corporate or 'mainstream' business. I see a gap in this world of prosperity. It's in the hands of people who barely know what a nervous system is, let alone what a regulated nervous system is. I want to put wealth in the hands of more

Wisdom of Wealth

women and create an era of filthy rich and famous abundant as fuck conscious women. My legacy will be my impact on the corporate world and my ability to weave worlds and bring the magic of being deeply connected to self and people of power. Or people who find themselves in positions of power that aren't seeking power in the first place, grounded in themselves, grounded in their spirituality and mission on earth. To usher in a new wave of consciousness and stewards, to allow prosperity to aid us in new ways and bring more harmony to how we live and do business.

About Lezly

Hi, my name is Lezly Kaye. I'm an accomplished professional with a diverse skill set, strategic expertise, and a holistic approach to change and performance. With over thirteen years of experience solving serious people problems, onboarding strategies and people performance, I recognised a significant gap in the market where sustainable long-term solutions were lacking. This realisation led me to create The Self Responsibility Code, a groundbreaking initiative that aims to transform how organisations view and engage with their employees.

Drawing on my own experiences as a business owner, I understand the challenges faced by organisations and entrepreneurs in attracting, retaining and enhancing the employee experience. I'm passionate about shifting the traditional mindset that treats employees as commodities, instead advocating for long-term plans that prioritise the well-being and growth of individuals, teams and organisations. My strategic expertise and training with prestigious organisations such as the Australian Institute of Company Directors (AICD) and the Australian Institute of Management (AIM) have sharpened my ability to navigate complex organisational challenges and drive meaningful results.

In addition to my strategic acumen, I pursued specialised education in disciplines such as Neuro-Linguistic Programming (NLP), hypnotherapy, breathwork, and nervous system regulation. These diverse areas of study have equipped me with a deep understanding of the human psyche, effective communication techniques and the importance of holistic well-being. By integrating this knowledge into my work, I have enhanced my ability to guide and advise businesses for sustainable change and performance. I understand that true transformation goes beyond surface-level strategies and addresses the underlying physiological and psychological factors that impact individuals and teams.

This comprehensive approach combines my strategic expertise with a holistic mindset. I empower organisations and individuals to take responsibility for their own success by nurturing a culture of self-responsibility, accountability, and continuous improvement. Through my unique blend of skills and experience, I guide businesses and grow teams in creating sustainable long-term solutions that enhance performance, foster well-being, and drive overall success.

I'm a visionary in the field of organisational development, recognised for my innovative and transformative impact. My strategic acumen, combined with specialised education, enables me to guide and advise businesses with a professional and strategic tone of voice while weaving in the holistic approach needed for sustainable change and team implementation.

You can connect with me hello@lezly.com.au

@lezlykaye

Martha Hansen

Anchoring Wealth Into Your Energy

Hi, my name is Martha Hansen. I've spent much of my career in personal development and wellness. I'm a practising coach, energy medicine practitioner, massage therapist, teacher and business owner. In my short time with you today, I'd like to give you a new way to begin thinking about how to manifest wealth of all kinds into your life using the power of your combined energetic and cognitive systems.

Let's start with some cognitive work and talk about wealth.

What is wealth anyway, and how can we experience more of it in our lives?

The Oxford Dictionary (OED) defines wealth as 'Prosperity consisting in abundance of possessions; 'worldly goods', valuable possessions, esp. in great abundance: riches, affluence.'

This definition aligns with what our Western and industrialised culture teaches about wealth: wealth equals possessing money, material goods and resources. Period! Unfortunately, this incomplete definition limits our ability to experience, create and attract wealth. While money, material goods and resources are definitely important aspects of wealth, they are by no means the be-all and end-all. So, let's complete the definition because words and their meaning matter.

My favourite definition of *wealth* lies in its original history. The *Online Etymology Dictionary* says that the word 'wealth' comes from the old English 'weal', which means wealth, welfare, and wellbeing. Weal is, in turn, related to the older word *wele*, meaning in a state of good fortune, welfare, or happiness. I love this and think it's the most empowering and holistic definition of wealth we can use: being in a state of good fortune, welfare or happiness.

Don't get me wrong, wealth is definitely related to dollars in the bank and the possession of assets that the *status quo* would have you declare on a tax return, especially in our industrialised society and the twenty-second century.

However, doesn't a certain amount of that create a state of good fortune, welfare or happiness for most of us? And, on the flip side, can't most of us think of someone who has a lot of money and material goods but wouldn't qualify for being in a state of good fortune, welfare or happiness? They may have money, but I would argue they don't have wealth.

When we limit our concept of wealth to what we put on our tax return or own a title to, we cap ourselves, our abundance, our happiness, and our life's potential. Wealth is a state of being, a state of mind, an essence and an experience as much as material goods. We can have a wealth of information, love, joy, experiences, community, support, relationships, opportunities and more. Don't we deserve to have all these things and more, not only the dollars in the bank account? Of course we do! That's the wealth we will permit ourselves to attract.

Before we go on, let's take a moment to talk about scarcity. Scarcity, particularly the mindset it creates, is the other side of the wealth coin. It's often the wall preventing us from experiencing *all* the wealth available to us.

The *OED* defines scarcity as 'Insufficiency of supply; smallness of available quantity, number, or amount, in proportion to the need or demand.' We can experience scarcity of almost anything in our lives: money, time, love, compassion, understanding, resources, opportunities, relationships and connection. The list is endless. Anything we have, we can also not have, feel like we don't have enough of, or we are doubtful we will ever have. In this way, scarcity is a genuine experience that many of us have lived and becomes a mindset or lens through which we come to view the world.

The most important thing to know about scarcity is that it is not a universal principle. It is a mindset. The universe and energy around you are ultimately abundant, kind and supportive. This doesn't mean we don't experience tremendous loss, hardships, discrimination, or challenges. It means that someone with a *wealth* mindset will emotionally, physically and psychologically weather these events entirely differently than someone with a *scarcity* mindset. The universe is always conspiring for our good.

I haven't met anyone who doesn't have the sneaky scarcity mindset creep in somewhere in their life experience. Myself included. I know people with zero scarcity mindset around income, yet believe there are only a limited number of good romantic partners and that all the good ones are already taken (scarcity).

Jumping to a view of scarcity is an instinctual survival response from our reptilian brain, and we aren't going to get rid of it anytime soon. However, we are these beautiful, complex mammals with prefrontal cortexes, and we do have the capacity to evolve and shift into new experiences of ourselves, our world and those around us. The calling you may feel towards increased wealth that inspired you to read this book is an excellent example of our unique ability to consciously evolve our survival instincts, which the scarcity mindset is part of.

Wisdom of Wealth

Let me share one of my favourite frameworks for understanding the complex interplay between our survival needs, our higher consciousness, and everything in between the chakra system. Specifically, I want to talk to you about Chakra One and how nourishing this aspect of our existence can profoundly affect how we experience, manifest, create and hold on to wealth.

The chakra system is rich and complex and would take thousands of pages to disseminate fully. To simplify how we will use it here, think of each chakra as different members of your energetic team working together to move you through your world and create your life. Each chakra centre has an area of expertise, focus and viewpoint offering different fears, needs, strengths, weaknesses and priorities. They work independently and in concert with the other centres for a common goal, like our digestive system. The stomach, small intestine, large intestine and gallbladder all have different roles but work together for absorption and elimination. Issues in the stomach will affect the small intestine, but the whole system keeps working—even with blockages present—towards absorption and elimination. Your chakra system works similarly.

In this way, wealth creation involves input from all seven chakra centres. However, when it comes to overcoming the scarcity mindset and fully believing that we deserve to experience a state of good fortune, welfare or happiness, aka wealth, Chakra One is where we need to start.

Chakra One is Represented by our Physical Environment

Everything around us is part of our first chakra, including our physical bodies. It's characterised by our relationship with the physical world and how we interact with form. It holds our basic right to be here and have. It's our foundation. As such, it's also ground zero for our self-nourishment and knowing, owning, experiencing and anchoring our *enoughness*.

Chakra One is also the last stop on the energetic manifesting channel, where dreams, visions, ideas, prayers, gifts, money and more come into literal form. Vitality in this energy centre is essential for manifestation and the subsequent rooting in and ability to hold on to and benefit from our manifestations.

To a degree, it doesn't matter how much money, abundance, or wealth by any other name we pull into our life through the rest of our energy system, if Chakra One is out of balance, we will experience some sort of adverse relationship with our right to exist, have, deserve and nourish ourselves. Without strength in these categories, we lose a solid foundation for the wealth we are creating to land on, take root in and flourish. For example, I'm sure we can all think of someone either personally or in the public sphere who makes money hand over fist and might even appear abundant or wealthy. However, they're still living with the same amount of scarcity, lack, insecurity, *not-enoughness,* and money stress as someone struggling to make ends meet. This is a Chakra One issue.

Is this An Area You Could Benefit from Working On?

To begin with, taking care of our foundation is never a waste of time. However, there are some possible signs that this energy centre may benefit from extra love and attention. Keep in mind, when faced with blockages, our system will respond in one of two ways: it will work harder or give up. In this way, imbalances often have a deficient or excessive quality.

For example, one person growing up with scarcity and lack of safety may respond with a fixation on material goods and do all they can to control their environment and protect themselves from the fear or anxiety of not having. Another person growing up in the same situation may respond by disowning their needs for material goods and feeling most comfortable in a vagabond-type existence to manage their fear or anxiety around not having. Imbalances in a person are difficult to generalise because they occur in your energy system in specific ways. That being said, here are a few possible signs of a Chakra One imbalance.

Wisdom of Wealth

- Financial Struggles.
- Chronic disorganisation.
- Anxiety.
- Poor focus.
- Hoarding.
- Rigid Boundaries.
- Poor Boundaries.
- Addiction to security.
- Fear.
- Material fixation.
- Dissociation from body.
- Obsession with controlling or managing body.

Lack of trust If you relate to any of the above, Chakra One and its inherent relationship with scarcity might be what's holding you back from experiencing all the wealth you desire. Don't be dismayed, though. You're already making a shift by simply reading this book. One of the best ways we can begin to work with Chakra One is a simple anchoring process, which I've included at the end of this chapter. You can then expand this process to align your system and pull in what you desire consciously.

Some days, you may want to complete steps one to four and allow your system to feel the balance of being grounded down and anchored up. On other days, you may want to continue through steps five to eight and work to consciously manifest and integrate new levels of wealth into your life.

Happy manifesting!

Free audio download of this meditation, please visit Wisdom of Wealth Auroracoaching (marthahansen.com).

Anchoring Your System and Calling in Your Wealth

- Find a comfortable position in a quiet and relaxed environment.

- Close your eyes and bring your attention to the centre of your stomach.
- Begin by taking a few deep breaths into your stomach and all the way down to your toes.
- Permit yourself to spend the next ten to twenty minutes with yourself and your inner world.
- Continue to breathe in and out in a steady rhythm throughout the duration of the exercise. Bring your awareness to the part of your body touching the floor, chair, or ground. Send all your awareness and energy to the connection between these two surfaces.
- Next, envision, imagine, or pretend that roots begin to sprout from your body and grow into the surface beneath you. Pretend, envision, or imagine them growing deeper into the floor, then into the earth beneath the floor, deeper and deeper. You might like to fill these roots with red light. Can you hear them crunching through the earth as they grow? Can you smell the soil as the roots wind deeper and deeper, rooting and anchoring? Notice you may have several larger, deeper roots going in different directions and smaller roots between them. Continue to send your roots out until they have grown far enough and deep enough for the nourishment and anchoring you need and deserve. Continue to keep this new root system in your awareness and bring your attention back to the centre of your body.
- Take a few deep breaths in and out, noticing what it feels like to breathe all the way down into your root system and back up to your core.
- On your next breath, we will begin expanding this root system into a tree.
- As you breathe in, envision, pretend or imagine that your breath carries the nourishment and support of the root system all the way up to your head, creating a solid tree trunk, anchoring back down

Wisdom of Wealth

into the earth with your next breath out. Continue to breathe this nourishment and support into the trunk and back down into the earth until it feels full of strength and stability.

- Next, take nourishment from your roots and up the trunk on your in-breath. Then imagine, pretend or visualise that your trunk is sprouting branches in all directions on your out-breath, reaching up towards the sky. You may even want to reach your arms into the air as you expand upwards. What leaves grow on your tree? Are they evergreen? Seasonal? In bloom? Let your awareness expand beyond the branches, up into the sky, the clouds and beyond. Allow yourself to feel the light and sun coming in through the branches as they blow lightly in the wind, flexible and strong.
- On your next in-breath, visualise this expansive light travelling down through the branches into the trunk, where you breathe it deep down into your roots, where it's converted into nourishment. Sit with this cyclical breathing for a minute or two until you feel the energy swirling out and anchoring up, then swirling back in and anchoring down.
- Bring your attention back to the centre of your body, noticing that the energy cycle keeps moving up and down.
- Now that you are anchored, you are going to invite into your system an awareness of the next right thing, person, energy, idea, vibration, or resonance that you'd like to have in order to create more wealth in your life right now. Trust whatever comes to you. It might be an image, a thought, an idea, or a feeling. It could represent anything from peace to a dollar figure, to an image of a tax accountant, to an inspiration. Trust whatever is coming is exactly the right thing for right now.
- Now, visualise, imagine or pretend that this exact next right thing is up above you in the sky, just waiting for you to call it down.
- On your next in-breath, allow yourself to travel from your roots,

up your trunk, up your branches and all the way up into the sky, wherever this *thing* awaits you.
- Open your arms, accept it into your system with willingness and gratitude and ask for it to return with you.
- When you feel ready, take a final in-breath, expanding into all the possibilities and on your out-breath, travel together back down through the sky into the leaves, the branches, the trunk and deep into the roots where this new thing, person, feeling, or idea turns red and becomes a part of your complex root system.
- You might even notice or imagine your root system expands or grows deeper as it becomes part of you.
- Complete this anchoring down as many times as it feels appropriate.
- You may go up and down only once or several times.
- Gently bring your awareness to the centre of your body and notice what it feels like to be this new version of you.
- Thank yourself, thank your energetic system, thank the universe, and thank the items you collected for the increased wealth you are creating in your life daily. Express gratitude for this new anchoring in and new way of being.
- When you are ready, open your eyes and take a deep breath, knowing you are actively calling in and anchoring in new levels of wealth.
- Feel free to capture on paper any realisations, ah-ha moments, ideas or actions that may have come to you during the exercise.
- Let yourself continue your day, knowing you have activated your first chakra manifestation powers.
- Do this as often as you'd like with as many different items that come to mind.

Be on the lookout for shifts in the world around you!
Happy manifesting!

About Martha

Hi, my name is Martha Hansen. I am an entrepreneur, coach, teacher and healer.

I own and manage Black Mountain Massage & Wellness (BMMW) an all-inclusive, body-positive massage and wellness clinic in Black Mountain, North Carolina. Additionally, I maintain a full spectrum healing and energy coaching practice with Aurora Energy Coaching & Massage and teach at the Center for Massage and Natural Health in Asheville, North Carolina.

I bring more than fifteen years of experience in the personal development, alternative health and spiritual growth fields to all my endeavours and find the intersections between mind, body and soul and the energetic and practical forever intriguing.

I have been studying money since my early twenties, which I consider just one important aspect of 'wealth', and I believe conscious capitalism

Martha Hansen

is most powerful when combined with business practices and values that focus on collaboration and cooperation rather than competition.

I believe we are in the middle of a great societal evolution around money, wealth and resources, and I am grateful to do my small part in contributing to this reorganisation. I am thrilled to be a member of this collaborative project focused on helping others tap into their own wealth creation capabilities and celebrate you for joining us in this new wealth paradigm.

When I'm not working or coming up with new philosophies on how to create more win-win-win business and money solutions in my private and personal life, you'll find me building things, gardening and taking care of the land I live on with my spouse, Kel, and our fur babies, Tatem, Buddy, Willow, Maya and KoraMay.

You can contact me at:
blackmountainmassageandwellness.com
marthahansen.com

Worksheets

Wisdom of Wealth

We at Maven Press hope you enjoyed all the wisdom shared by our beautiful authors

Sometimes mapping out and designing how you want to manifest wealth can be daunting. So, to help you on your journey and provide a giudeline or template to work from, we've added some handy worksheets.

If you would like a printed version, I personally like to stick my manifestations where I can see them, just copy the link below.

Happy planning your future!

www.mavenpress.com.au/the-wisdom-of-wealth

Worksheets

DAILY PLANNER

DATE: / /

07:00
08:00
09:00
10:00
11:00
12:00
13:00
14:00
15:00
16:00
17:00
18:00
19:00
20:00
21:00

REMINDERS

SHOPPING LIST

MEALS

WATER INTAKE

MOOD TRACKER

QUOTE OF THE DAY:

Wisdom of Wealth

WEEKLY PLANNER

MONDAY
_____
_____
_____
_____

TUESDAY
_____
_____
_____
_____

WEDNESDAY
_____
_____
_____
_____

THURSDAY
_____
_____
_____
_____

FRIDAY
_____
_____
_____
_____

SATURDAY
_____
_____
_____
_____

WEEKLY GOALS
_____
_____
_____
_____

SUNDAY
_____
_____
_____
_____

Worksheets

MONTHLY PLANNER

MONTH

BIG DATES

_____

_____

_____

NOTES

_____

_____

_____

Wisdom of Wealth

SELF-CARE CHECKLIST

	M	T	W	TH	F	SA	SU
Drink a glass of water to start the day	☐	☐	☐	☐	☐	☐	☐
Enjoy 45 minutes of exercise	☐	☐	☐	☐	☐	☐	☐
Get some fresh air	☐	☐	☐	☐	☐	☐	☐
Have a healthy breakfast	☐	☐	☐	☐	☐	☐	☐
Enjoy a warm morning drink	☐	☐	☐	☐	☐	☐	☐
Plan out your day in your planner	☐	☐	☐	☐	☐	☐	☐
Stretch your body	☐	☐	☐	☐	☐	☐	☐
Take regular breaks	☐	☐	☐	☐	☐	☐	☐
Enjoy some sunshine	☐	☐	☐	☐	☐	☐	☐
Take hot/cold bath or shower	☐	☐	☐	☐	☐	☐	☐
Read something meaningful	☐	☐	☐	☐	☐	☐	☐
Play some invigorating music	☐	☐	☐	☐	☐	☐	☐
Disconnect	☐	☐	☐	☐	☐	☐	☐
Eat a healthy snack	☐	☐	☐	☐	☐	☐	☐
Wind down by avoiding bright light at night	☐	☐	☐	☐	☐	☐	☐
Get in bed before 10 pm	☐	☐	☐	☐	☐	☐	☐

Worksheets

SMART GOALS

WHEN SETTING GOALS, MAKE SURE IT FOLLOWS THE SMART STRUCTURE. USE THE QUESTIONS BELOW TO CREATE YOUR GOALS.

SPECIFIC
WHAT DO I WANT TO ACCOMPLISH?

MEASURABLE
HOW WILL I KNOW WHEN IT IS ACCOMPLISHED?

ACHIEVABLE
HOW CAN THE GOAL BE ACCOMPLISHED?

RELEVANT
DOES THIS SEEM WORTHWHILE?

TIME BOUND
WHEN CAN I ACCOMPLISH THIS GOAL?

Wisdom of Wealth

DAILY GRATITUDE

/ /

TODY I'M FEELING

POSITIVE AFFIRMATIONS

TODAY I'M GRATEFUL FOR

1. _____
2. _____
3. _____

SOMETHING I'M PROUD OF
_____

MORE OF THIS:	LESS OF THIS:

MY FAVORITE MOMENT THE DAY
_____

TOMORROW I LOOK FORWARD TO
_____

Worksheets

GRATITUDE

MONTHLY PREVIEW

/ /

THIS MONTH'S INTENTION IS

_____
_____
_____

HOW DO YOU FEEL?	HOW DO YOU WANT TO FEEL?

WHERE DO YOU WANT TO FOCUS YOUR ENERGY?

_____
_____
_____

Notes

_____
_____
_____

Wisdom of Wealth

GRATITUDE

MONTHLY REVIEW

/ /

HIGHLIGHTS OF THE MONTH

1. _____
2. _____
3. _____

WHAT IS SOMETHING NEW YOU'VE LEARNED?

_____
_____
_____

WHAT WERE SOME OF THE CHALLENGES YOU FACED?

_____
_____
_____

WHAT IS THE BEST THING YOU HAVE DONE FOR YOURSELF THIS PAST MONTH?

_____
_____
_____

HAS PRACTICING GRATITUDE HELPED YOU THIS MONTH?

| YES | MAYBE | NO |

Worksheets

Weekly Planner
Manifest and Attract

I am aware and grateful for:

_____

_____

My main intention for the week

Affirmations for myself

Thoughts to meditate on

_____

_____

_____

Wisdom of Wealth

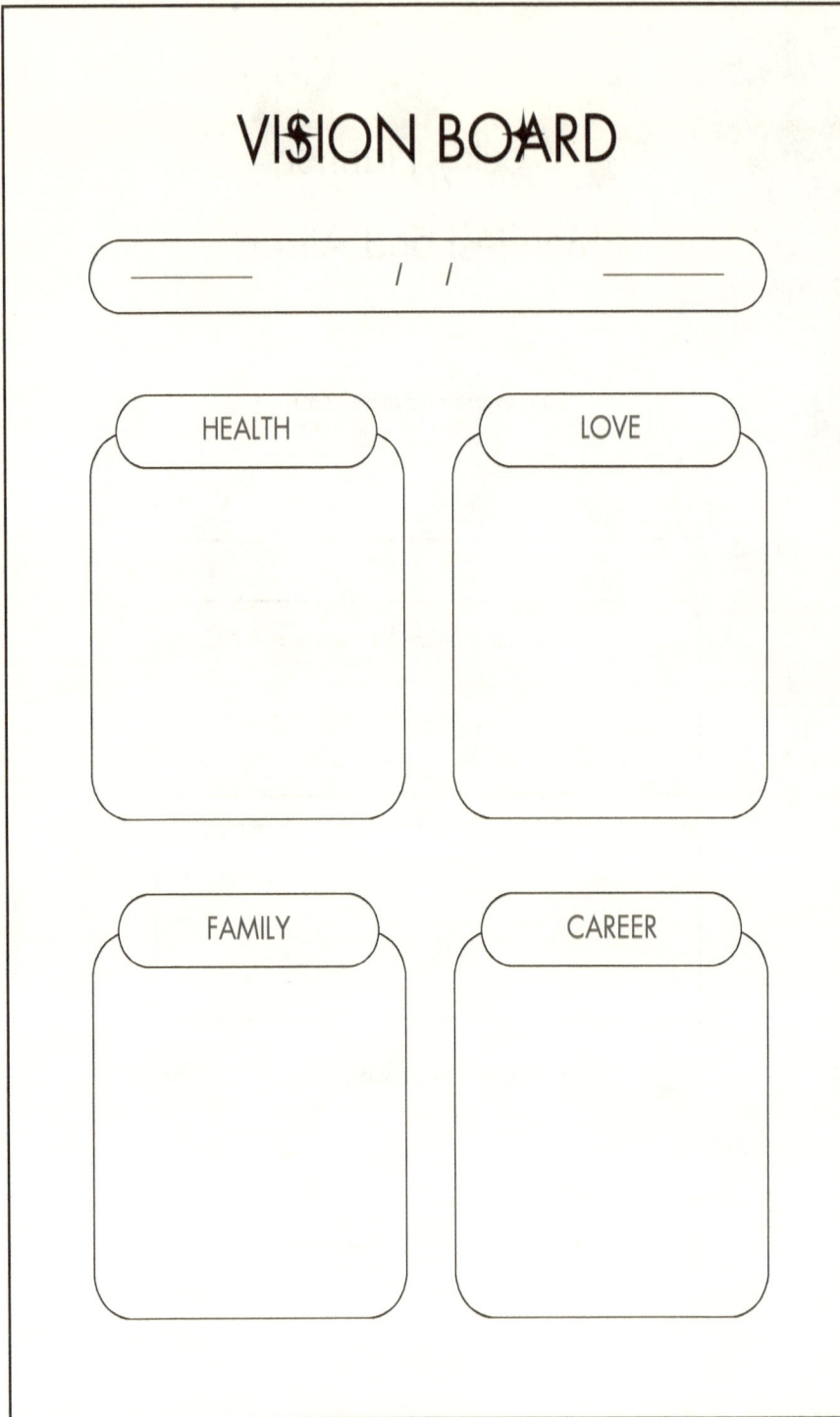

Worksheets

MONTHLY BUDGET

Month: _____

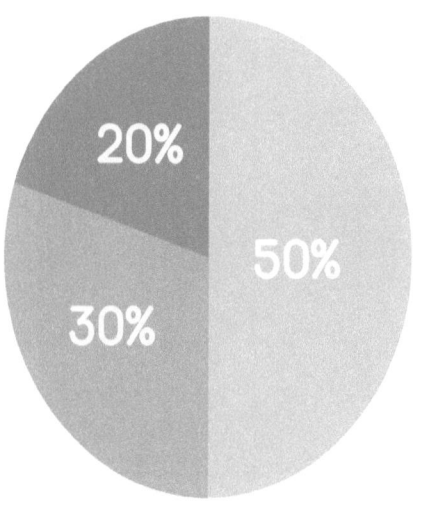

Income

Cost	%		
Living	50%		
Saving	30%		
Playing	20%		

www.ingramcontent.com/pod-product-compliance
Lightning Source LLC
Chambersburg PA
CBHW022020290426
44109CB00015B/1254